THE CENTERED
LEADER

THE CENTERED LEADER

Maximizing Influence through Personal Transformation

THE SHE CENTER

GOOD
MEDICINE
PRESS

For permissions, contact info@goodmedicinepress.com

Published by Good Medicine Press
Santa Fe, NM 87506
https://goodmedicinepress.com

ISBN: 978-1-967446-00-1

Library of Congress Control Number: 2025935817

Edited by Steele Campbell
Cover design by Kels Quinn

This is a work of nonfiction. While all attempts have been made to verify the information provided, the author does not assume any responsibility for errors, omissions, or contrary interpretation of the subject matter herein.

Printed in the United States of America

Centered Series, Book 1, The Centered Leader

goodmedicinepress.com

When my daughter was 7, we went out to a nice dinner in the midst of an executive conference. Surrounded by scores of business men all in suits, drinking and networking, my daughter watched for a moment then spun her chair to face me and said, "I'm a Boss, too."

-Lydia Knight
Founder of The She Center

This book is dedicated to women of every age and stature.

May you never lose the light of knowing
your destiny is to lead.

INTRODUCTION

A SHIFT FROM OLD WAYS

We find ourselves at a crucial turning point. The rigid, hierarchical style of competitive leadership that has dominated for so long is on its way out. The time has come to bid farewell to any approach that stifles creativity, hinders progress, or perpetuates gender biases. We stand on the precipice of change, and quite frankly, it is long overdue. The world is shifting, as it does, and if we want to have a say in how the new landscape will be formed, we must listen well. Only then can we truly lead.

The statistics of change are all around us. Did you know that approximately 80% of divorces are initiated by women? This is not merely a number; it rings a resounding wake-up call. Did you know the 4B movement that shifted social structures and gender expectations in South Korea has spread worldwide, taking deep root in the United States where the passivity of going with the flow has been replaced with self-determination and communities that are rejecting the roles society projects? Women are stepping away from marriages, careers, beauty standards, societal expectations, and other facets of their lives that no longer serve them. They are reclaiming their autonomy and actively seeking something more meaningful, whether it be in their personal lives or careers. This seismic shift is indicative of a larger movement, one that recognizes the fundamental need for alignment between our values, our life's pursuits, and the profound recognition that how we spend our time is how we spend our lives.

The desire for autonomy and flexibility in how we lead and work and who we choose and heed as leaders worthy of our attention has become a fundamental aspiration. We crave an environment that allows all of us to unleash our full potential and to contribute in ways that align with our unique strengths and passions. The traditional, one-size-fits-all leadership model can no longer accommodate the myriad of diverse talents and aspirations within our global workforce.

When women assume leadership positions, teams become more innovative and also more resilient. It is not solely a matter of gender balance; the inclusion and integration of diverse perspectives fosters an environment of heightened creativity, adaptability, and problem-solving. Beyond the impact on team dynamics and business practices, women also wield significant economic influence through their spending decisions and thus shape substantial portions of consumer demand. There is a novel approach to leadership that, when embraced, increases team loyalty, reduces employee turnover, and increases profit. It isn't a reproduction or regurgitation of the control-and-command leadership that has brought us this far. The future is marked by leadership that embraces soft skills and diverse voices and which centers around inclusion, validation, and celebration.

Women and men have already begun to say "no" to the limitations and constraints imposed by outdated leadership paradigms. They are bravely voting with their feet, making the courageous decision to leave behind jobs and situations that feel restrictive, unfulfilling, or misaligned. It is now our collective responsibility to seize this moment and revolutionize leadership. We must embrace a new paradigm that celebrates and empowers the strengths of every individual. The time has come to break free from the shackles of division and forge a path towards unity through diversity.

This book offers insights into the journey of becoming a Centered Leader, a comprehensive approach that encompasses not only traditional leadership skills but also empathy, collaboration, and the ability to inhabit inclusive environments. Embracing Centered Leadership will require us to confront and dismantle existing biases, confront privilege, and challenge the status quo. Yet it is only through these transformative efforts that we can collectively build a world where leadership transcends differences of identity and embraces the unique and valuable qualities within each and every one of us.

This book is for everyone of every stripe: not limited to class, race, preference, or gender. This book is inclusive and celebrates all modalities of being. But more so, this book is for anyone who wants to unlock the leadership potential in themselves and others by centering their leadership from within. It is from that place of uplifting difference and championing inclusivity that we all rise. Let us embark together on this journey, where leadership, when rooted in compassion, authenticity, and an unwavering commitment to achieving holistic success, becomes a force that unites us in progress and celebration.

CHAPTER 1

IT STARTS WITH YOU: LEADING SELF TO LEAD OTHERS

Of course, you may be thinking, it starts with you. After all, you are the one reading this book. As you seek a new pathway to becoming a Centered Leader, your choice to engage with these ideas already demonstrates your commitment to growth and your willingness to examine and transcend the barriers of unconscious bias we all carry.

While countless qualities contribute to effective leadership, research consistently shows that great leaders share several fundamental traits. A comprehensive Harvard Business Review study examining over 17,000 leaders found that the most effective leaders excel in three core areas:

- Self-awareness and emotional regulation.
- Strategic thinking combined with decisive action.
- The ability to inspire and empower others.

These qualities don't emerge from position or title—they grow from a Centered Self. When you lead from a robust and actualized

Center, authentic strength emerges, genuine power develops, and your leadership illuminates more than your own path forward, brightening the journey for everyone within your sphere.

As we begin this journey together, let's start with celebration—as we do in every She Center practice. Take a moment to celebrate your commitment to growth, your openness to new perspectives, your awareness of your leadership and the responsibility that it carries, and your courage to examine your own beliefs and behaviors.

The journey to Centered Leadership isn't about becoming someone else—it's about unlearning that which is not truly you to uncover your authentic self and deepen your self-awareness.

Self-awareness is the cornerstone of personal development and authentic leadership. It involves a deep understanding of your emotions, strengths, weaknesses, and values. By objectively observing your thoughts, actions, and reactions, you gain clarity about who you are and how you show up in the world.

The ancient Greeks captured this fundamental truth when they inscribed "know thyself" above the passageway to the inner sanctum of the Oracle at Delphi. Modern research validates this ancient wisdom. Harvard Business Review studies show that leaders with high self-awareness lead teams that perform up to 33% better than those with lower self-awareness. Organizations with strong senior leadership teams practicing regular self-reflection show nearly double the profitability of their competitors.

Self-awareness operates on two distinct levels. Internal self-awareness encompasses understanding your own values, passions, aspirations, and impact on others. External self-awareness involves understanding how others view you and your effectiveness as a leader. Both dimensions are essential for a Centered Self from which to lead.

The path to self-awareness requires honest assessment of your thoughts, actions, and impact. As you develop this awareness, you'll make more conscious choices, respond rather than react, and lead with greater authenticity.

Being aware of your internal scope is to understand on a deeper level your emotional home and reactions—your emotional intelligence, which is vital to becoming a Centered Leader.

Emotional intelligence involves recognizing, understanding, and managing your emotions while empathizing with the emotions of others. Developing emotional intelligence enables leaders to navigate complex interpersonal dynamics, resolve conflicts, and build genuine connections with team members. It also creates a supportive and inclusive work environment.

Recent studies show that leaders with high emotional intelligence create teams with 20% higher productivity and 87% lower turnover rates. While EQ has become somewhat of a catchphrase, at The She Center, we find that much growth work is rooted in emotional intelligence. The most successful leaders demonstrate this intelligence through consistent awareness of team dynamics, thoughtful responses to challenges, and the ability to inspire trust even in difficult situations.

We know that change is not possible without adopting a growth mindset. Even the best coach can't help if you don't believe your attributes and behaviors, even those deeply engrained, can evolve. All the information in the world could fall on barren ground without the fertile mind open to accepting growth and change. Stanford psychologist Carol Dweck's groundbreaking research in her book, *Mindset*, shows that leaders with a growth mindset are three times more likely to reach their higher potential than those with a fixed mindset.

Having a growth mindset means viewing challenges, setbacks, and failures as opportunities for learning and development. When you embrace this perspective, you understand that your abilities, intelligence, and capacity for leadership can strengthen through dedication and deliberate practice. This outlook encourages you to tackle new challenges, seek feedback, and pursue continuous improvement. When you demonstrate a growth mindset, you inspire your team to approach their own challenges with resilience and curiosity.

Centered Leadership requires vulnerability and authenticity. This means bringing your true self to each interaction, even when it feels uncomfortable or risks judgment. By embracing vulnerability, you create space for genuine connections with your team. When a leader admits uncertainty or shares past failures, it gives others permission to do the same. You build an environment where individuals feel safe to express their authentic selves, leading to deeper trust, natural collaboration, and breakthrough innovation. Centered Leaders inspire courage not through perfection, but by openly sharing their experiences, aspirations, and challenges. This transparency creates an atmosphere where growth feels both possible and natural.

In pursuing your authentic Center, developing healthy self-care routines and mindfulness practices is essential. Research from the Corporate Leadership Council shows that leaders who maintain consistent mindfulness practices make decisions with self-reported more clarity in over 22% of responses, and 35% report significant change in managing stress more effectively.

Mindfulness practices—be they brief meditations, thoughtful journaling, or simple breathing exercises—nurture a deeper self-awareness and presence. These practices help you remain present and attentive to both your needs and others. At The She Center, we've seen how even five minutes of mindful practice before key meetings can transform a leader's presence and decision-making.

This inner work offers clarity and peace for our movements and intentions. While this topic deserves its own volume, the essential truth remains: practicing self-care recharges your energy and maintains a sustaining and sustainable work-life balance. When you prioritize your own well-being, you create an unspoken permission for your team to do the same, fostering continuous high performance.

Becoming centered is a lifelong journey of learning and growth. This journey isn't linear—it spirals upward, revisiting familiar challenges with new wisdom. From a Centered Self, your clearest decisions and most impactful leadership qualities emerge. Centered Leadership develops through dedication to acquiring knowledge and skills, and by challenging existing perspectives. This might mean studying emerging leadership trends, mastering new technologies, or understanding shifting cultural dynamics.

Maintained curiosity expands your horizons and allows natural adaptation to our rapidly evolving business and social landscapes. The most effective leaders dedicate significant time to learning: both individually and with mentors, coaches, and an affirming community. As the world changes and places new demands on every leader, dedication to growth ensures a solid center and ascending spiral of Centered Leadership.

These core tenets of centered development form the bedrock of authentic self-leadership. Research from the Center for Creative Leadership reveals that leaders who master these fundamentals are twice as likely to create high-performing teams and sustain long-term organizational success. This increases efficiency, productivity, and employee retention, maintaining organizational knowledge key to lasting success.

To recap these formative principles: becoming the leader of your ultimate potential requires deep self-awareness that guides decisive action, emotional intelligence that builds genuine connections, a growth mindset that transforms challenges into opportunities, and authentic vulnerability that inspires trust and permission for innovation.

By prioritizing self-care, cultivating mindfulness, and embracing continuous learning, you evolve naturally as a leader while inspiring others to reach their full potential. When you lead from a truly Centered Self, you allow your Sphere to center around you and your organizational ambitions, building a culture where growth and collaboration develop organically and where people feel appreciated and empowered. A movement with a Centered Leader at its heart consistently blossoms into an extraordinary combination of organizational achievements and personal fulfillment.

Remember, the journey to Center can be as long as it is satisfying and fruitful. It isn't perfect. Moving forward often means recognizing which steps not to take as much as which to follow, and failures should be appreciated for the learning experiences they are. All of this is progress. Centered Leadership from a Centered Self will strengthen your team, your Sphere, and the impact of your organization, and it will contribute toward building a Centered World. Your personal elevation will lift those around you in seen and unseen ways.

REFLECTIONS

1. **Leadership Baseline**: Consider a recent leadership challenge. How did you respond emotionally, mentally, and physically? What would your response look like from a more centered place?

2. **Authenticity Assessment**: Where do you feel most authentic as a leader? Where do you feel you're still wearing a mask? The gap between these two states often reveals your next growth opportunity.

3. **Commitment to Center**: What one small practice could you begin tomorrow to strengthen your leadership center? Remember, transformation happens through consistent small actions rather than grand gestures.

CHAPTER 2

THE ROOT OF THE PROBLEM IS THE KEY TO THE SOLUTION

Often, when we reflect on the trajectory of our lives and the outcomes we desire, we confront a fundamental truth: our thoughts govern our actions, which in turn shape our results. Neuroscience confirms this connection. Research from Norman Doidge's seminal book on neuroplasticity, The Brain that Changes Itself, shows that recurring thought patterns create neural pathways that directly influence our behavioral choices—as Donald Hebb famously put it, "what fires together wires together."

The key to transforming our lives lies in altering our actions. Yet here's where many leaders stumble: they attempt to modify their actions without addressing the root cause—their deeply ingrained and often subconscious thought patterns. This noble but misguided effort creates a cyclical battle, like driving down a road with deep ruts. You can try to avoid the ruts by holding to the edge, but any slip lets the rut take the wheel, which only deepens it further. The solution isn't avoiding the ruts—it's repairing the path. Understanding this dynamic is the first step toward genuine transformation.

Our thought patterns, especially those operating beneath conscious awareness, wield tremendous power. These hidden patterns nest within the depths of our habits and unquestioned beliefs, influencing our decisions and actions without our conscious recognition.

Here lies an enigma of self-development: While we may genuinely believe ourselves to be compassionate and fair-minded individuals aligned with principles of equality—and while in many ways this might be true—our actions can sometimes unintentionally perpetuate institutional biases, racism, or distorted perceptions that contradict our professed values. Unexamined beliefs can blind us to how our actions might affect others or silence certain voices. A leader might advocate for diversity while unconsciously favoring familiar perspectives in meetings. Another might champion innovation while unconsciously shutting down ideas that challenge traditional approaches.

When these beliefs remain unexamined, it is easy to miss their impact. Social attitudes evolve rapidly in our connected world, unmasking previously accepted behaviors as problematic. Consider early Disney movies: though well-intentioned and meant for children's entertainment, they contain scenes now recognized as stereotyping, dehumanizing, and improper. This makes unveiling our hidden thought patterns not just important, but imperative for effective leadership.

To effect true transformation, we must illuminate the murky depths of our subconscious mind and bring these thought patterns to the surface where they can be examined clearly. When we address these root causes, profound shifts occur. A leader who discovers an unconscious bias against remote workers, for instance, can consciously reconstruct that belief based on performance data rather than physical presence.

No matter how deeply ingrained a belief may be, we can dismantle these habitual thought patterns and construct a new blueprint for our actions. With a Centered Self as our objective, this internal work extends beyond personal growth—it shapes organizational culture and societal progress. The key lies in embracing our understanding of the brain's intricate workings and learning to effectively collaborate with it.

At The She Center, our work freeing thousands of women from the shackles of eating disorders has revealed a powerful truth: lasting transformation occurs when we equip ourselves with the necessary tools to confront and reshape deep-seated thought patterns. With these thought-reprogramming structures, our clients achieve sustainable change at rates which confound the traditional medical model.

By engineering our thought habits, behaviors like binge eating— long seen as an incurable disease—can be entirely eliminated from our actions and thoughts, even after decades of reinforcement. The secret lies in understanding that our thought patterns, while often operating beyond our conscious control, exert remarkable influence on our actions.

This principle applies robustly to leaders across industries, where centering leadership can reshape ingrained habits that no longer serve. A micromanaging executive can shift to empowering leadership. A conflict-avoidant manager can develop healthy confrontation skills. The key lies in understanding that our thought patterns, while operating beyond conscious control, can be systematically rewired.

To break free from limiting patterns, we must retrain the brain's reward system. By interrupting the automatic feedback loop and establishing new neural pathways, we achieve what appears miraculous to traditional approaches. This methodology applies equally to transforming leadership behaviors—whether improving emotional regulation, enhancing decision-making, or strengthening team communication.

The process is clear: identify the automatic thought pattern, interrupt the cycle, establish new neural pathways, and reinforce positive changes. Through this approach, we've guided thousands from perceived helplessness to centered strength, proving that with the right tools, any leader can fundamentally redesign their automatic responses and emerge stronger.

Drawing guidance from the grandfather of neuroplasticity, Dr. Donald Hebb, and his foundational work, The Organization of Behavior, we access our brain's natural capacity for change. What is now known as Hebb's Rule proves that neurons repeatedly fired together create stronger connections—much like a path through a forest becomes clearer with each crossing or the rut we want to avoid grows deeper with each reinforcement, the new path we want to follow grows easier with repetition.

When we consciously recognize and question outdated thought patterns, we begin rewiring our neural circuitry. A leader who automatically responds to disagreement with defensiveness can learn to pause, listen, and engage constructively instead. With each repetition of this new response, the neural pathway strengthens while the old one weakens through disuse.

This process requires courage—stepping away from familiar patterns feels uncomfortable at first. Yet each time we disrupt an unhelpful pattern and choose a more empowering response, we strengthen new neural connections that align to center.

The landscape of leadership begins with a clear vision, filling in old ruts, and becoming grounded in what we aspire to embody. By embarking on a path of self-reflection and training the mindset, beliefs, and habits we desire, we can align our actions with a vision of a more equitable and cohesive culture. This alignment requires three key elements: authentic self-reflection, deliberate training of new mindsets and habits, and consistent practice that turns aspirations and effortful action into automatic responses.

Through deliberate and sustained efforts, we become catalysts for change and can construct a world that aligns with our deepest values. The most effective leaders demonstrate this through small, daily choices rather than grand gestures—choosing curiosity over judgment, collaboration over competition, inclusion over expedience.

To create this world we seek, we need conscious, aware leaders who have done the internal work and who act and react from a balanced center. This lofty aspiration can be elusive, but like climbing any mountain or crossing any vast terrain, the journey begins with a single step.

REFLECTIONS

1. Pattern Recognition: Think of a recurring challenge in your leadership. What automatic thoughts arise? Notice these thoughts without judgment, simply observing. How might these thought patterns influence your leadership decisions?

2. Value Alignment: Identify three core values you believe guide your leadership. Now recall your actions from the past week. Where do you see alignment? Where do you notice gaps? What thought patterns might be creating these gaps?

3. Commitment to Change: Identify one small but significant thought pattern you're ready to transform. What daily practice could you implement tomorrow to begin rewiring this pattern?

CHAPTER 3

THE WOMAN IN THE MIRROR: REFLECTIONS ON LEADERSHIP

In leadership, we engage in a complex dance of perception and response. Our actions ripple through our organizations, creating waves that return to us through others' responses. This is a cognitive as well as perceptual response, described in French philosopher Jean-Paul Sartre's concept of being-for-self and being-for-others. We must balance these dual beings by recognizing how others perceive us while also staying true to our authentic core.

When we lead, we must lead authentically, knowing that people respond to our entire presence, not just to our directives. A leader's energy is contagious—an anxious leader often creates an anxious team, while a confident leader tends to inspire calm. This dynamic is known as the "mirroring effect"—where our own unresolved challenges often surface within our team's behaviors. For example, a leader who struggles to delegate might find their team reluctant to take initiative. Observing reactions to us as a mirror serves as a powerful diagnostic tool, revealing where we need to focus our personal growth to become centered and lead more effectively.

The mirroring effect manifests in two distinct ways: direct mirroring and inverse mirroring. Understanding these patterns helps us recognize our leadership impact more clearly.

Direct mirroring occurs when the internal struggles we grapple with are mirrored back to us through our team's behaviors. Organizational psychology research reveals this effect moves throughout the team, including among peers. For example, if we find ourselves struggling with time management, we might see our team struggling with deadlines. If we dismiss someone's input, they might start dismissing others' ideas because our behavior has sanctioned it.

These patterns can emerge in countless ways, even when we are not aware we are displaying an uncentered self. Leadership anxieties are especially infectious—when a leader quietly worries about job security, the whole team can start doubting their own value and future.

Direct mirroring works like holding up a mirror that reflects our own challenges, showing how deeply leadership influence flows downward. Parents see this clearly with children, who mirror both our best and worst moments—especially those actions and reactions we hoped they wouldn't notice. Our mindset and energy are contagious, whether positive or negative.

Inverse mirroring reveals a more subtle leadership pattern—we overcompensate to mask our fears and concerns. Studies show over half of senior managers experience this phenomenon, often unknowingly. Many of these patterns emerge from good intentions: a formerly micromanaged leader becomes too hands-off, a supervisor who struggled with harsh feedback becomes reluctant to offer constructive criticism, or a previously unsupported leader exhausts themselves supporting others. Leaders who have internalized a deep responsibility for their team's success might avoid delegating work, fearing they'll overwhelm their team. While well-meaning, these responses can prevent team growth and drain the leader's energy.

The mirroring effect often triggers self-doubt, making us question our own abilities as leaders and creating false barriers. When we see our unresolved issues reflected in our team or catch ourselves overcompensating, it is a common reaction to feel like an imposter or to doubt one's calling to lead. These doubts typically surface in predictable patterns: "If I can't manage my own time perfectly, how can I lead others to better efficiency?" "If I sometimes struggle with conflict, how can I guide my team through difficulties?" "What if they discover I'm still learning, too?"

We might hesitate to embrace new leadership roles, thinking we must first resolve our own problems. Yet here lies a powerful paradox: Acknowledging these very human struggles often strengthens, rather than weakens, leadership. When a senior executive openly shares their work-life balance journey, it creates psychological safety for their team to address similar challenges, paving the way for more effective and Centered Leadership.

The goal isn't perfection—it's leading authentically through your own growth journey. Here we emphasize again that becoming a Centered Leader starts with leading ourselves first—in every way. A 2022 article published in the National Library of Medicine confirms that leaders who actively invest in their own development and   self-care have teams who report greater well-being. This self-leadership requires three essential components: tools to recognize and regulate our patterns, skills to navigate these challenges on a personal and professional level, and support systems for continued growth.

Through dedicated self-leadership, we can create a strong foundation of authenticity, trust, and empathy within our team. An uncentered leader can disrupt team balance, affecting both morale and productivity. Compare a leader practicing emotional regulation and creating space for thoughtful responses with one acting reactively and spreading stress.

The message here is clear: our internal state directly shapes our external impact. When we prioritize our center, we create the environment for our individual and collective excellence.

Remember, the practice of leading ourselves is more than improving our ability to lead others; becoming one others seek to follow is about creating an environment where authenticity and growth thrive. Every effective leader must do their own work first, both in actions and mindset.

When we prioritize self-reflection, we lay the foundation for a more cohesive and successful team dynamic. The Center we develop within ourselves becomes the model for a Centered Sphere of influence. It cannot be overstated that the well-being and success of our team begins with our own Centered Self.

Take a few moments with these reflections on your journey to center. Avoid overthinking, allowing yourself to respond quickly and honestly, and write down your thoughts. These notes will mark the start of your Centered Leadership path.

REFLECTIONS

1. **Mirror Recognition:** In the past month, what patterns, direct and inverse, have you observed in your team that might reflect your leadership state? Consider both successes and challenges.

2. **Trust through Transparency:** Where have you held back from sharing your own growth journey with your team? Reflect on one area where appropriate vulnerability might strengthen your leadership. What small step could you take toward more authentic sharing?

3. **Leadership Support Network:** Who helps you see your blind spots? Every leader needs both peers and mentors who can recognize patterns we miss in our own reflection. Consider: Where might you expand your leadership community? What qualities would you seek in a coach who could help you recognize and transform these patterns?

CHAPTER 4

CASE STUDIES: THE POWER OF A NEW PARADIGM

MISSING BRIJHETTE

Brijhette exemplifies the transformative power of Centered Leadership. As a senior leader in a Fortune 500 corporation, she guides a team who respects her expertise and draws inspiration from her genuine leadership approach. Since joining her company, she has earned multiple raises and promotions—not through aggressive self-promotion, but by delivering measurable results through consistent, Centered Leadership.

Her journey with The She Center demonstrates how authentic leadership naturally attracts recognition. While many leaders chase advancement, Brijhette focused on developing her Center and bringing her whole self to her role. This authentic approach has consistently attracted rewards and advancement opportunities.

Throughout the years, we've witnessed Brijhette transform obstacles into growth opportunities. Even as her influence grew, her willingness to remain coachable illustrates a fundamental truth about Centered Leadership: the strongest leaders never stop learning and evolving.

Yet Brijhette's career path hasn't always been smooth, revealing challenging realities many face in corporate America. Despite holding advanced degrees and an impressive track record, her early career hit a puzzling wall of rejection. She applied for positions matching her qualifications and followed every recommended step in the application process, only to face consistent rejection. The pattern was clear, though its underlying reason remained frustratingly obscure.

Determined to uncover the root cause of her struggles, Brijhette conducted a revealing experiment. She began submitting her identical resume under the name "Bridget"—a more traditionally Anglo-Saxon spelling of her name. She removed her photo from applications, and when images were required, she altered her appearance to minimize her identity as a woman of color, even taking the drastic step of shaving her natural hair.

This painful compromise illuminates the very biases that Centered Leadership must address. Brijhette's experiment wasn't just about advancing her career—it documented how unconscious bias systematically excludes talented leaders from organizations, ultimately diminishing workplace diversity and innovation.

The swift positive response to these changes struck Brijhette with bitter clarity. Job offers began arriving for "Bridget"—the same candidate with identical qualifications, differentiated only by presentation. This contrast exposed the deep-rooted bias lurking, often unnoticed, in hiring decisions.

Brijhette's story then takes a powerful turn. Through her work with The She Center, she recognized that her unique perspective and experiences weren't limitations to minimize—they were assets to leverage. She boldly brought her authentic self to leadership, incorporating her cultural background, diverse viewpoint, and natural presence.

As Brijhette embraced Centered Leadership, her organization began to recognize and reward her distinctive contributions. Her authentic leadership style opened doors to greater responsibilities, elevated titles, and fair compensation. More significantly, she blazed a trail for others to follow, demonstrating how Centered Leadership can transform both individual careers and organizational cultures.

While Brijhette's journey reveals the obstacles faced by marginalized individuals, it also offers hope. She found a company that truly aligns with her values and provided an environment where she could flourish as a leader. Where she once worked four jobs to make ends meet, she now thrives in a single role that fully recognizes her worth.

Now, her team's genuine admiration and respect for her shine through in everything they do. Their appreciation extends beyond formal recognition, showing up in spontaneous gestures of respect and gratitude. This natural appreciation demonstrates how Centered Leadership naturally cultivates loyalty and engagement.

The company recognizes and celebrates Brijhette's value through numerous raises and promotions. We're proud to celebrate her outstanding achievements in The She Center mastermind coaching group, Rise. Her experience shows that when organizations embrace authentic leadership, everyone benefits: Leaders can fully express their gifts, teams become more engaged, and companies retain exceptional talent.

Brijhette's story reveals the power of a new leadership paradigm that prioritizes inclusivity, diversity, and fairness first. Her experience challenges organizations to go deeper than surface-level diversity initiatives, to examine hidden biases, and to create an environment where everyone can truly succeed, regardless of their background. By adopting this more enlightened leadership approach, organizations can unlock their diverse talent's potential and thereby drive growth, innovation, and excellence.

While we celebrate Brijhette here and rejoice that her value has finally been seen, countless others still face marginalization from persistent organizational biases in corporate culture. Brijhette initially had to hide herself to blend in before she could shine. The fact that she needed to mask her identity to gain entry speaks to deeply rooted patterns in corporate culture that continue to limit potential and stifle innovation.

Moving toward Centered Leadership requires more than celebrating individual success stories. It demands that all leaders actively address biases by scouring hiring practices for hidden barriers, creating environments where authenticity and difference thrive, and building systems that recognize diversity as a source of strength.

In the world of leadership, Brijhette's experience challenges us to reevaluate our hiring processes and their inherent biases. It is crucial to acknowledge that talent is talent, regardless of race, gender, sexual preference, or ethnic background. This is not just a personal matter: By overlooking potential in individuals like Brijhette, organizations miss out on exceptional talent.

Brijhette's rise to senior leadership demonstrates a valuable truth: Centered Leadership transcends conventional success metrics. Her story elucidates how authentic leadership, when finally recognized and supported, naturally evolves into increased responsibility and influence. Yet this evolution shouldn't require leaders to first mask their identity. True organizational excellence emerges when companies build environments where diverse leadership styles and perspectives can flourish from day one.

Research shows that companies with diverse leadership teams consistently deliver stronger innovation, better decision-making, and deeper market understanding. But beyond these measurable benefits lies a more fundamental truth: Centered Leadership creates workplaces where everyone can contribute their full talents while staying true to themselves.

KATHI IN THE MIRROR

Kathi's journey to Centered Leadership began in an unexpected place—through confronting her relationship with control. As a successful doctor and business owner, she managed complex medical cases and ran a thriving practice. Yet beneath this professional success, she grappled with binge eating disorder, a struggle that revealed deeper patterns affecting her personal and professional life.

Her drive to micromanage her household and practice reflected an inner battle with control. While she maintained strict order in her professional realm, her relationship with food remained chaotic. This discord created a leadership blind spot that strained her relationships with family and staff alike.

When Kathi finally sought help for her binge eating, she opened the door to profound insights about leadership, control, and authentic power. By addressing this personal challenge, she unknowingly embarked on a journey of self-transformation.

When Kathi sought coaching from The She Center, she believed she didn't have binge eating disorder (BED)—she was too controlled. Her professional identity as a doctor had become both shield and obstacle. She meticulously scheduled binges every eight days to avoid a BED diagnosis, which was technically defined as purging once a week. This intellectual manipulation revealed how even highly accomplished leaders can use their strengths to maintain patterns that no longer serve them.

Her transformation occurred when Kathi brought the same dedication to her healing that she brought to her medical practice. Rather than using her knowledge to maintain denial, she applied it to understanding her true capabilities. She embraced the coaching process, approaching personal change with the same scientific rigor she brought to treating patients.

The speed of her transformation—freedom from bingeing in just three days—highlighted a crucial leadership principle: When we stop using our strengths to maintain our struggles and instead apply them to growth, breakthrough becomes possible. This shift from resistance to engagement would later inform how she tackled leadership challenges.

In less than half a week, she experienced what previously seemed impossible: complete liberation from decades of compulsive binge eating. With this new freedom came a profound shift in her emotional and mental well-being. She discovered an inner strength and determination she hadn't known existed. Where she once felt controlled by triggers and urges, she now wielded practical tools for mastering her responses.

This newfound emotional mastery transformed her presence as a leader. She discovered that the same principles that freed her from binge eating—recognizing patterns, challenging automatic responses, and choosing new behaviors—applied directly to managing her clinic. With her primary struggle resolved, Kathi turned her analytical mind to examining other ingrained patterns that no longer served her.

She approached her leadership habits with fresh eyes, asking crucial questions: Which behaviors truly served her team? Which reactions stemmed from old triggers rather than present needs? This systematic review of her leadership style from a more Centered Self revealed opportunities for growth she hadn't previously recognized.

As Kathi mastered the art of self-leadership, her transformation rippled through every relationship in her life. The shift began at home with her teenage children, who became the first to experience her new, centered approach. Where she once micromanaged details of their lives—mirroring her professional control tendencies—she now created space for their autonomy.

Her children felt more empowered to take ownership of their own lives and began to make confident, self-fulfilling decisions. The foundation of their relationship shifted from control to connection. Family discussions evolved from directive to collaborative, from tension to trust. The relationship between Kathi and her children blossomed, fueled by authenticity, enjoyment, and a genuine desire to support each other.

In her medical practice, Kathi's transformational journey had a remarkable impact, becoming a living laboratory for Centered Leadership. Through open communication, vulnerability, and a commitment to continuous learning, she cultivated an environment of collaboration, empathy, and personal growth. Rather than maintaining the traditional hierarchical structure common in medical practices, she created collaborative spaces where every team member's voice mattered.

Her willingness to show appropriate vulnerability as a leader—acknowledging when she didn't have all the answers—gave her team permission to bring their whole selves to work. This authenticity sparked a cultural shift where continuous learning and growth became part of the practice's DNA. Each team member felt empowered and valued, contributing their unique perspectives to greater collective success. Her team became more productive and found deeper satisfaction in their increased impact.

Patients noticed the positive changes, too. The team's heightened engagement and empathy led to higher patient satisfaction. In an era of rushed, impersonal medical care, her practice stood out. Patients responded to the distinctive atmosphere—how every staff member, from the front desk to the examination room, brought both professional expertise and genuine presence to their roles. The practice became known throughout the medical community as a haven of compassionate care, attracting both patients seeking a different healthcare experience and talented professionals eager to work in an environment valuing clinical excellence and human connection.

Kathi's journey showed how personal transformation can catalyze organizational change. By understanding her own capacity for change, she developed a deeper appreciation for others' potential. This insight allowed her to create an environment where everyone—staff and patients alike—could access their capacity for growth and healing. Her practice became living proof that when leaders transform themselves, they create space for others to do the same.

Kathi's evolution as a Centered Leader opened new horizons in patient care. Moving beyond traditional approaches, she began integrating her understanding of transformation into her treatment protocols. Her acceptance into Dr. Joe Dispenza's exclusive health professional training program marked another milestone in her journey to reimagine healthcare delivery. This expansion reflected a deeper truth: True healing encompasses both physical health and personal transformation. When reflecting on her journey, Kathi acknowledged that her ability to pioneer this integrated approach grew directly from her work with The She Center's principles, community, and coaching—resources that helped her first transform herself before transforming her approach to medicine.

Kathi's journey from a successful doctor masking inner struggles to a self-leading, transformational leader is a testament to the power of standing in one's power as a Centered Leader. Her willingness to confront her own challenges created a foundation for authentic leadership that transformed both her practice and her profession. By addressing the root causes of her own patterns, she developed an intuitive understanding of how personal growth catalyzes organizational change.

Her story demonstrates that when leaders commit to their own transformation, they create environments where others naturally embrace growth and change. What began as a personal journey to overcome binge eating became a powerful testament to how Centered Leadership can revolutionize an individual practice, enhance the experience of patients and healthcare providers, and offer greater care in a more empowered environment.

CHAPTER 5

BECOMING A CENTERED LEADER

Contrasting traditional patriarchal leadership with newer, inclusive leadership reveals key insights about becoming a Centered Leader. Traditional models, proliferated greatly during the industrial age as remnants of pre-industrial, feudal power structures, relied heavily on rigid top-down control. These hierarchical systems treated workers as replaceable parts in a machine, valuing compliance over contribution and authority over authenticity. Such environments naturally breed toxicity: fear suppresses innovation, silence substitutes for honest dialogue, and survival instincts overpower collaboration.

Today's organizational challenges require a fundamentally different approach. While traditional leadership creates walls, Centered Leadership builds bridges. Where old models demanded uniformity, Centered Leadership celebrates individual contributions. This approach is about validating the humanity that is within each team member and helping both organizations and people reach a higher potential.

Traditional patriarchal leadership resembles a fortress—rigid, isolated, and defensive to anything not already within its walls. At its core often sits a dominant figure, typically male, who guards power like a scarce resource. These leaders view authority as a zero-sum game where sharing power means losing it. These leaders may prioritize their own interests and maintain control through fear and intimidation, suppressing diverse voices until silence passes for agreement and conformity masquerades as harmony. This approach crushes creativity and innovation, forcing teams to find congruence only in echoing the dominant perspective.

Centered Leadership, however, reimagines organizational power dynamics. It treats diversity not as a corporate initiative but as a competitive advantage. Centered Leaders understand that different perspectives illuminate blind spots, test assumptions, and lead to better decisions. They create spaces where team members can bring both their professional expertise and unique life experiences to the table.

Instead of commanding from above, Centered Leaders orchestrate talent—coordinating contributions, amplifying quiet voices, and ensuring all perspectives get heard. This leadership style generates better solutions, increased innovation, and deeper team engagement. It creates an upward spiral, cultivating a culture where creativity flourishes and innovation reigns.

A powerful example of encouraging individual creativity is Google's "20% time" policy, where employees dedicate one day per week to passion projects outside their core responsibilities. It was met with favor from the employees and has resulted in the creation of Gmail, now the world's leading email service, and AdSense, the user-directed advertising platform generating billions in revenue for Google's parent company, Alphabet.

Centered Leadership thrives on active listening and gathering input from team members across all levels. Evolved leaders recognize that they don't have all the answers and that their team's collective wisdom is their most valuable asset. This approach requires the humility to acknowledge limitations and the skill to weave diverse perspectives into effective solutions.

By creating psychologically safe spaces, Centered Leaders encourage open dialogue where employees feel secure sharing novel or untested ideas without fear of failure. They recognize that when team members worry about judgment or repercussions, valuable insights remain unspoken. By creating a Centered Sphere where every voice can ring true, these leaders help their organizations reach peak performance.

Centered Leaders cultivate balanced awareness while championing equity and fairness throughout their organizations. Their influence radiates from their own centered state, positively shaping their immediate teams and eventually their entire organizational cultures. They take deliberate action to identify and address systemic inequalities, starting with the courage to confront their own unconscious biases.

This dual focus on Centering Self and then Sphere transforms surface-level diversity initiatives into meaningful cultural change. Instead of merely hitting quotas or making declarations, these leaders create authentic pathways for underrepresented individuals to advance into leadership roles. They recognize that true inclusivity emerges at the intersection of self-awareness and social responsibility. From this foundation, leaders build lasting meritocratic systems that recognize and reward talent in all its forms, ensuring every team member has genuine opportunities to contribute and grow.

One essential practice of becoming a Centered Leader is developing and cultivating self-awareness. This awareness forms the gravitational center from which all other leadership qualities emerge and consists of a committed practice of examining one's strengths, weaknesses, and emotional patterns with unflinching honesty.

When leaders operate from this examined center, they naturally distinguish between knee-jerk reactions and thoughtful choices, understanding how their personal history, cultural conditioning, and professional experiences shape their leadership approach. This awareness enables them to choose responses that benefit both their team and the organization's broader goals.

Through developed self-awareness, Centered Leaders recognize their limitations and biases before these internal barriers affect their decisions. This awareness creates a pause—a moment of non-judgmental reflection from which to observe both internal reactions and external situations. From this vantage point, leaders can distinguish between their own projections and the actual needs of their team.

This self-awareness transforms how leaders handle workplace dynamics. When addressing team conflicts, they separate personal biases from the situation at hand. When facilitating discussions, they notice their pre-conceived notions and actively adjust for them. While this level of self-knowledge doesn't completely eliminate challenges, it provides leaders the internal stability to better address complex situations with clarity and purpose. Their center becomes a compass for authentic action rather than reactive response.

Understanding traditional leadership methods while consciously choosing a different path requires both wisdom and courage. A Centered Leader must maintain their stable core even amid organizational turbulence. This becomes especially challenging in environments where aggressive behaviors and the silencing of dissent are not just tolerated but encouraged. The pressure to conform to established patterns can shake a leader's commitment to operating from center.

The challenge intensifies when organizations actively reward behaviors that contradict Centered principles. A leader might see aggressive tactics earn promotions while thoughtful, inclusive approaches go unrecognized. Yet this apparent contradiction presents Centered Leaders with their greatest opportunity for impact.

Where traditional leadership relies on authority, Centered Leadership draws strength from genuine collaboration. This shift appears in clear, observable changes: Decisions now flow through all levels of the organization rather than just downward, gathering wisdom and building shared commitment. The competitive drive that once pitted colleagues against each other transforms into a culture of mutual support and collective achievement.

The scarcity mindset which fortresses traditional leadership—where success is viewed as a limited resource to be hoarded—gives way to an abundance perspective under Centered Leadership. This shift moves beyond simple win-lose metrics to focus on more meaningful measures: team development, sustainable growth, and shared accomplishments. Instead of isolated leaders pursuing distant dreams and a plethora of demands, Centered Leadership creates an environment where everyone's success contributes to the whole.

The contrast between control-focused, traditional leadership and flexible, Centered Leadership becomes crucial in today's fast-paced business world. When facing uncertainty, traditional leaders often respond by tightening their grip on processes and decisions, unintentionally limiting their organization's ability to adapt. Centered Leaders, grounded in a stable foundation, maintain flexibility without losing direction. This balanced approach allows them to share control while keeping the organization on course.

Flexibility shows its value in daily operations. Centered Leaders evaluate ideas based on merit rather than source, allowing innovation to emerge from any level of the organization. Their strong foundation helps them stay open to new approaches while maintaining a clear sense of purpose. This blend of stability and adaptability works especially well during major changes, enabling quick shifts while keeping teams aligned and engaged.

Traditional leadership often manifests as a high-stakes gamble, where leaders take bold risks while maintaining careful distance from potential failure. When initiatives succeed, these leaders step forward to claim credit; when efforts fail, they shift responsibility downward to their teams. This pattern reveals the instability of ego-driven leadership, where personal reputation overshadows organizational health.

Centered Leaders take a different approach to risk and responsibility, making decisions through a balanced integration of data, intuition, and collective wisdom. They lead from genuine strength which emerges from emotional intelligence rather than emotional distance. While traditional leaders might mistake stoicism for strength, Centered Leadership recognizes that real power comes from staying grounded while fully engaging with challenges. This integration of head and heart, logic and empathy, produces leadership decisions that serve the entire organization rather than individual egos.

Centered Leaders demonstrate their strength by mastering and effectively channeling their emotions. This mastery manifests in authentic responses that welcome the full range of human experience in professional settings, inspiring team members and encouraging discretionary effort. Where traditional leaders often respond to emotional team members with detachment or dismissal—treating feelings as organizational inconveniences—Centered Leaders view emotions as valuable data points, create safe spaces for processing feelings, and celebrate the wholeness of a person.

They build environments where appropriate emotional expression becomes a strength that can inform and transform both individuals and organizations. This acceptance of human wholeness in the workplace doesn't compromise professional standards; instead, it enhances effectiveness by empowering people to bring their full capabilities to their work.

Centered Leaders fundamentally reimagine organizational power structures, serving as stewards of their team members' talents and aspirations. Gone are the days of success being measured in completed tasks. Instead, this leadership approach values personal growth, human skills, and the holistic health of the organization, transforming hierarchical authority into a cultivation of human potential. While toxic leadership creates rigid boundaries between roles, Centered Leadership recognizes the interdependent nature of organizational success.

The impact of Centered Leadership often manifests as increased loyalty, higher job satisfaction, and stronger commitment to organizational goals. Team members under Centered Leadership demonstrate greater ownership of their work and pride in their contributions. When their identity is valued, doing great work becomes part of who they are. From the mail clerk to the CEO, the Centered Leader's approach celebrates each position as vital to the success of the whole, where employees naturally invest more of themselves in their work, creating a self-reinforcing cycle of achievement and satisfaction.

Moreover, Centered Leaders don't isolate themselves in the clichéd ivory towers. Instead of maintaining unassailable authority, they actively cultivate relationships that challenge their assumptions and support their growth. This network typically includes mentors who have walked similar paths, coaches who provide guidance and maintain accountability to Centered principles, and trusted advisors who offer unfiltered feedback about blind spots and development opportunities.

These strategic support relationships provide essential external perspectives on leadership challenges, create safe spaces for processing complex decisions, and maintain the leader's commitment to continuous development. The willingness to remain coachable while leading others distinguishes Centered Leadership from traditional approaches. By actively engaging with their own growth edge, Centered Leaders model continuous development and inspire their teams to follow their example with enthusiasm.

In addition to focusing on their own growth, Centered Leaders also prioritize developing their team members. They invest in their growth, providing opportunities for learning and encouraging their team to tackle new challenges. These leaders recognize that individual autonomy drives organizational success and sustainability.

Centered Leaders balance their own development with the creation of an environment where team members can expand their capabilities and influence. This dual focus transforms growth from an occasional training event into a core part of organizational culture. Through varied development opportunities—from formal coaching to stretch assignments—these leaders actively build organizational capacity from within.

When leaders emphasize individual growth, they unlock new levels of organizational resilience. Empowered team members who develop their unique strengths and exercise real autonomy help create adaptable organizations. By supporting authentic individual development rather than enforcing conformity, leaders unleash their teams' innovative potential and creative problem-solving abilities. Tired hierarchical structures can evolve into dynamic networks of confident contributors who drive success through both individual and collective achievements.

By embracing these practices, Centered Leaders build internal fortitude that radiates outward, inspiring those around them. They spark meaningful change by decentering outdated leadership models and creating fresh approaches that are more inclusive, collaborative, and compassionate.

Teams flourish under leaders who model resilience rather than demonstrate rigidity, who invite participation rather than demand compliance. When leaders fully embrace their center, they illuminate the path for others to discover their own leadership potential.

To truly embody center, leaders must bridge the gap between understanding and action, weaving core principles into their daily decisions. They translate abstract concepts into tangible behaviors that their teams can see and follow. While many organizations claim to value inclusivity and equality, Centered Leaders actively demonstrate these principles through consistent, purposeful action. Their everyday actions create clear patterns where small decisions compound into significant impact, showing teams that Centered Leadership thrives in practice, not just in theory.

Creating an inclusive and equitable environment requires deliberate effort to dismantle systemic barriers and establish fair policies. Centered Leaders confront outdated practices directly, replacing them with equitable solutions. They examine organizational structures with fresh eyes, identifying hidden biases that lurk in familiar processes.

Centered Leaders make psychological safety their priority, recognizing that innovation blooms only when people feel secure enough to share their full perspectives. They cultivate environments where team members can bring their whole selves to work without fear of judgment. This means actively valuing and respecting diverse viewpoints, encouraging open dialogue, and addressing conflicts constructively. By nurturing a culture of trust and inclusivity, Centered Leaders empower their teams, which naturally enhances performance and drives innovation.

Another critical aspect of Centered Leadership is mindful decision-making. Centered Leaders make conscious choices based on careful reflection and awareness of how their decisions impact both individuals and the organization. They actively seek input from all stakeholders and weigh different perspectives before making informed decisions. This thoughtful approach helps them avoid impulsive or biased judgments that may perpetuate inequality or harm team members.

Centered Leaders also spotlight team achievements with genuine appreciation, knowing recognition powers engagement. They specifically identify individual contributions and connect team members' actions to organizational success. This detailed attention transforms routine praise into meaningful recognition, which many employees consider essential for job satisfaction.

When leaders recognize unique contributions with a mindset of communal success, they build belonging and deepen ownership of duty. Team members who feel valued and heard invest more deeply in shared goals. Centered Leaders inspire a culture of inclusion and recognition, and they become the cornerstone of essential team dynamics. Their authentic appreciation creates a self-reinforcing cycle: Recognized people naturally recognize others, cultivating an environment where every contribution matters. The journey to becoming a Centered Leader is a lifelong one, marked by continuous self-reflection, growth, and an unwavering commitment to creating positive change through inclusive leadership.

Frances Hesselbein modeled this process in her transformation of the Girl Scouts of America, demonstrating that success comes from consistently embodying these principles in daily actions and decisions. As the first leader outside the founding family, Hesselbein revolutionized the organization by focusing on inclusion and mission rather than tradition. During her thirteen-year tenure, she doubled minority membership and transformed a declining organization into a modern leadership development powerhouse—all while maintaining her core belief that "leadership is a matter of how to be, not how to do."

Today's Centered Leaders follow a similar path of purposeful action, recognizing that each decision either strengthens or weakens their leadership center. Even small choices made in haste accumulate into lasting impact. The way they conduct Monday meetings, address team conflicts, or respond to setbacks shapes both their leadership influence and organizational culture, demonstrating the importance of acting from a centered place every day.

Centered Leaders shape their organizations and communities through positive influence. Their teams solve problems more creatively, adapt to challenges more readily, and collaborate more effectively. When leaders operate from center, they unlock hidden potential in others. Team members stretch beyond their comfort zones, take calculated risks, and develop capabilities they never knew they possessed.

Centered Leaders multiply their impact by awakening leadership potential in others. Hesselbein demonstrated this principle through her work with the Girl Scouts, where she firmly believed that every girl deserved leadership training, regardless of their background. Under her guidance, the organization actively developed future leaders across all socioeconomic and racial backgrounds. This approach to leadership becomes contagious—when team members witness the effectiveness of Centered Leadership firsthand, they naturally begin applying these practices in their own roles. The result is an organic leadership pipeline, where authentic example inspires others to embrace their own potential and work toward creating a more just and equitable society.

In an increasingly diverse and interconnected world, Centered Leadership isn't just a choice; it's a necessity. Hesselbein proved this when she revitalized the Girl Scouts into a modern leadership incubator. Rather than maintaining traditional hierarchies, she implemented a more fluid, circular management system that encouraged innovation at every level. Her success demonstrated that organizations clinging to outdated command-and-control models struggle to keep pace, while those embracing centered practices thrive. These forward-thinking organizations consistently attract ambitious talent, retain valuable team members, and adapt swiftly to change. Their success stems from the collective strength of people empowered to lead from their own centers.

The journey to center echoes far beyond the individual leader. Like a stone dropped in still water, the impact of Centered Leadership creates expanding circles of influence. Each leader who commits to this path sets in motion patterns of positive change that touch every corner of their organization.

The benefits of centering one's self and leadership style emerge in both measurable and immeasurable ways. Center-led teams exceed performance targets, spark innovation, and drive revenue growth. Yet the deeper impact shows up in quieter moments—when a team member steps confidently into their potential or feels safe enough to propose a creative new solution. Organizations transform from mere workplaces into spaces where people discover their best selves.

The investment in finding one's center yields returns that compound daily. Each centered decision builds trust, each authentic interaction strengthens connection, and each moment of genuine leadership inspires others to lead. Through this ripple effect, Centered Leadership creates thriving ecosystems of human potential where business success flows naturally.

REFLECTIONS

1. **Growth Edge Identification:** Examine your current leadership style and your aspirational Centered Leadership practice. Which aspect of Centered Leadership feels most natural to you? Which presents the greatest challenge? What is one shift that could create significant positive change?

2. **Resistance Recognition:** Consider where you encounter the most resistance to Centered Leadership—both internal and external. How do you maintain your center when facing traditional leadership expectations? What strategies help you stay centered under pressure?

3. **Sustainable Success:** Where do you see evidence of sustainable success in your organization? Examine the specific connection between Centered Leadership practices and lasting positive outcomes. How might strengthening your center amplify these results?

CHAPTER 6

BUILDING A SOLID FOUNDATION

Today's business landscape demands unprecedented leadership agility. With the influx of AI, the advancement of women in leadership at every level, and customers prioritizing integrity, efficiency, and sustainability, leaders must adapt and embrace change. The traditional, patriarchal leadership models that dominated the 20th century—with their rigid hierarchies and command-and-control approaches—are crumbling in the face of technological and social evolution.

Katherine Graham's journey at *The Washington Post* in 1963 offers valuable insights. Despite pressure to maintain conventional leadership patterns, Graham recognized that success required a fresh approach—one emphasizing consultation over command and inclusion over authority.

Graham's evolution from a hesitant widow to a confident publisher who guided *The Post* through the Pentagon Papers crisis showcases the power of Centered Leadership. Rather than relying on traditional displays of power, she built her foundation on authentic strengths: careful listening, collaborative decision-making, and an unwavering commitment to truth. Her success proved that traditionally feminine leadership qualities—once dismissed as weaknesses—actually create stronger, more resilient organizations. Today's Centered Leaders follow this path, building foundations sturdy enough to weather uncertainty yet flexible enough to embrace change.

WOMEN'S ROLE IN LEADERSHIP

No discussion on Centered Leadership would be complete without highlighting the crucial role that women play in driving change and fostering inclusive, sustainable organizations. Katherine Graham's transformation of *The Washington Post* offers more than an inspiring story—it provides a practical blueprint for organizational evolution. When Graham assumed leadership, she faced dual challenges: leading a major newspaper while confronting an industry that openly doubted women's capacity to lead. Her response revolutionized the *Post* and journalism itself.

The business case for women's leadership extends far beyond individual success stories. The Peterson Institute's comprehensive study of 21,980 companies reveals a compelling pattern: Organizations with women in key leadership positions consistently outperform their peers. Companies with strong female leadership demonstrate higher profitability, stronger employee retention, and more sustainable growth patterns, with some achieving increased profit margins of up to 25%.

This success stems not from women adopting traditional leadership styles with a different face in the same position, but was birthed from bringing authentically feminine strengths to the executive suite—collaborative decision-making, inclusive communication, and long-term thinking. By embracing women's unique insights and experiences, organizations unlock innovative solutions and tap into a vast pool of previously underutilized talent.

The strengths Graham relied upon to captain *The Washington Post's* culture—deep listening, relationship building, and intuitive understanding of team dynamics—created lasting competitive advantages. She recognized the value of communal knowledge and sought advice from unlikely sources. Abandoning a top-down flow of knowledge, she used active listening to collect the wisdom of seasoned professionals that held experience if not titles and direct control. She knew she did not hold all the answers, and also knew she didn't have to in order to lead effectively. Her leadership style demonstrated how combining empathy with moral courage drives historic change, setting a powerful example for future generations of leaders.

Leadership studies consistently reveal these distinct strengths. Women leaders typically score higher in emotional intelligence, show greater adaptability during crises, and build more resilient teams. Yet all is not lost for our male counterparts. This isn't about gender superiority—these powers stem from a willingness to lead from centered strengths and to embrace collective wisdom rather than conform to traditional power structures. When organizations value such leadership qualities, regardless of whether they come from women or men, they create cultures where both productivity and employee satisfaction flourish.

A CENTERED FOUNDATION

Madam C.J. Walker's rise from washerwoman to America's first self-made female millionaire demonstrates how Centered Leadership builds lasting foundations. In the early 1900s, when society systematically excluded women—especially women of color—from business leadership, Walker created an empire by leading from her authentic center. She built her success by genuinely connecting with her community, deeply understanding her customers' needs, and courageously sharing her own hair loss journey.

Walker developed her Centered Leadership without formal education. Born to former enslaved people, orphaned at seven, and married at only fourteen, she instead learned from her peers and freely shared her knowledge, knowing that others' success would lift her as well. In an environment where she couldn't vote or attend school, she mastered what modern leadership now refers to as the "soft skills" or "human skills" of authentic vulnerability, deep-level communication, and genuine care for both employees and customers.

Her beauty schools trained thousands of women, weaving practical skills with leadership development. Walker's declaration, "I had to make my own living and my own opportunity...but I made it," demonstrates how centering oneself and leading from a solid foundation can center one's Sphere and create a cascade of new leaders.

Madam C.J. Walker understood that personal transformation drives business success. She invested heavily in her sales agents' development through "training conferences" that went beyond product knowledge to include personal development, financial literacy, and political activism. Like Walker's schools, The She Center recognizes that traditional business education often overlooks crucial leadership elements—the human skills that transform good managers into Centered Leaders.

These skills demand more than intellectual understanding; they require deep personal work and consistent practice. Walker demonstrated this when she insisted her agents become community leaders as well as salespeople, telling them, "I am not merely satisfied in making money for myself, I am endeavoring to provide employment for hundreds of women of my race." Today's Centered Leaders follow this same path, recognizing that their personal growth catalyzes the development of others. The She Center builds on this powerful legacy, providing the education we should have had—comprehensive training in vital human skills integral to sustainable success.

Walker modeled centered vulnerability by openly sharing her own hair loss journey with customers and sales agents. Rather than hiding this personal challenge, she transformed it into the cornerstone of her business and leadership philosophy. Her openness created deep trust—customers believed in her products because she had lived their struggles. Her sales agents, many facing similar challenges, found inspiration and courage in her example.

Centered Leaders today follow this pattern of strategic vulnerability. They understand that true strength comes not from projecting perfection, but from creating authentic connections. When a leader admits to wrestling with a difficult decision, team members feel safe voicing their own uncertainties. When leaders share lessons from their setbacks, teams become more innovative, knowing that imperfect attempts are better than safe silence.

Walker's success flowed largely from her mastery of deep-level communication. She listened beyond her customers' and agents' words to understand their underlying dreams and struggles. At her annual conventions, she created forums where women could speak freely about their challenges—both personal and professional. This deep listening helped her build a trusted product line and a movement that enriched lives.

Deep-level communication requires an open heart and focused presence. Centered Leaders tune into the undercurrents beneath surface conversations: unvoiced fears that stifle innovation, the unspoken dreams awaiting encouragement, and quiet wisdom that could solve ongoing challenges. When team members experience this depth of attention, they bring their full intelligence to challenges. Ideas flow more freely, collaboration emerges naturally, and solutions arise from unexpected sources. This deep, centered communication morphs traditional reporting relationships into partnerships built on real understanding and shared purpose.

Madam C.J. Walker exemplified leadership through genuine care for her team's total well-being. "I am not merely satisfied in making money," she insisted to her agents. She lived these words through action—creating educational opportunities, supporting political activism, and teaching wealth-building strategies. When her sales agents succeeded, she celebrated beyond their sales figures, highlighting their personal transformation into community leaders and independent businesswomen.

Today's Centered Leaders continue this tradition of holistic care. They understand that team members bring their whole selves to work—their dreams, struggles, and untapped potential. These leaders design development plans that align career goals alongside personal aspirations. They spot signs of overwhelm and step in before burnout hits. They celebrate births, offer support during losses, and acknowledge how life events affect work performance. This authentic attention to human needs creates an environment where people naturally strive for excellence.

The best leaders admit they don't have all the answers and seek quality coaching to fuel personal and professional growth. Even Walker turned to mentors, including successful Black entrepreneurs like Robert Wood and white businessmen willing to share market insights. She then made coaching a cornerstone of her business model, creating a network where experienced agents mentored newcomers. This approach built a leadership pipeline that created opportunities for thousands of women.

Guidance accelerates growth. Centered Leaders actively seek coaches and mentors who challenge their assumptions and illuminate blind spots. The most effective leaders both receive and provide coaching, creating continuous chains of development throughout their organizations. This dual role—being both student and teacher—keeps leaders growing while multiplying their impact. Regular coaching helps leaders stay centered during challenges, make decisions aligned with their values, and create environments where others can rise into their full leadership potential.

Walker understood the power of community, turning her annual conventions into what she called "the gathering of the eagles."

These groundbreaking gatherings gave women leaders a place to share strategies, celebrate successes, and support each other through challenges—where each woman's success lifted others. At her first convention in 1917, Walker told her agents, "I had to make my own living and my own opportunity...but I want you to take these opportunities I create and make them better."

Modern Centered Leaders similarly thrive in strong communities. They seek spaces where they can speak honestly about their challenges. In these communities, leaders find support from others who understand their journey and who celebrate their growth alongside them. Whether through peer groups, virtual gatherings, or regular coaching like that which The She Center provides, these communities become intimate spaces to learn, share, and grow. In the right community, vulnerability transforms from risk to strength, failures become learning opportunities, and individual growth multiplies into collective wisdom.

Leadership continues to evolve at an accelerating pace. Staying effective requires continuous learning and adaptation. Centered Leadership demands we bring our whole Selves to our work, just as Walker brought her personal hair loss struggle to her business vision. This authenticity gives others permission to do the same, inspiring teams to respond with increased trust and engagement. By mastering the heart of Centered Leadership—authentic vulnerability, deep-level communication, and genuine care—leaders create cultures of psychological safety where innovation naturally emerges.

Walker's enduring legacy teaches us that Centered Leadership adapts to change while remaining anchored in timeless principles. Her famous words, "Don't sit down and wait for the opportunities to come. Get up and make them," continue to inspire today's leaders as they tackle modern challenges. By blending authentic leadership with practical action, Walker created a blueprint that remains relevant in our fast-paced business landscape.

A CENTERED AND AUTHENTIC SELF

When leaders center themselves in authenticity, they root themselves in their true self. This level of self-awareness demands self-alignment—a state where internal values, external actions, and organizational goals flow from the same source. Like a compass needle always turning toward true north, Centered Leaders develop an internal guidance system that helps them navigate complex decisions with clarity and purpose.

The centered state isn't static but rather a dynamic balance leaders actively maintain. When pressured to compromise values for quick wins, Centered Leaders pause to reconnect with their core principles. When faced with difficult decisions, they consult their internal compass before checking spreadsheets. By consistently returning to center, they create a pattern of leadership others trust because they sense its authenticity. Teams choose to follow Centered Leaders because they witness the power of decisions made from genuine conviction rather than convenience.

Centered authenticity breaks from the scarcity mentality that often prevails in leadership paradigms. While uncentered leaders hoard power and recognition as finite resources, Centered Leaders embody a non-scarcity mindset. They understand that shared power multiplies, distributed recognition energizes, and expanded opportunities create more for all.

This shift from scarcity to abundance thinking reshapes organizational culture. Centered Leaders build environments where success has no limits. They actively celebrate team achievements, knowing individual growth strengthens the whole. They amplify voices sharing breakthrough insights and create space for team members to stretch beyond their usual roles. This abundance mindset feels better and often leads to increased innovation, stronger collaboration, and sustainable growth without team burnout.

Authenticity requires vulnerability—the courage to be imperfect in an image-obsessed world. Trying to project perfection actually diminishes impact. Instead, Centered Leaders demonstrate real strength by quickly acknowledging mistakes, sharing lessons learned, and welcoming feedback even when it might sting. This authentic approach doesn't weaken their authority; it deepens it.

In crucial moments, this plays out clearly: Centered Leaders own their part in project setbacks rather than seeking scapegoats. They openly acknowledge challenges while maintaining confident progress through uncertain territory. When team members raise difficult questions, they respond with genuine consideration rather than defensiveness. This blend of vulnerability and strength creates teams willing to take smart risks and offer honest feedback, trusting their insights will be valued rather than punished. Authentic leadership turns traditional notions of strength upside down, revealing how power flows from genuine connection, not artificial perfection.

Authenticity and diversity form a natural partnership in Centered Leadership. When leaders bring their whole selves to work—including historically undervalued aspects of their identity—they empower others to value their own unique experiences and perspectives. This authenticity extends beyond surface-level inclusion to embrace the full spectrum of human experience, thought patterns, and problem-solving approaches that diversity brings.

Centered Leaders actively cultivate environments where different perspectives productively collide. They know innovation rarely emerges from comfortable agreement; it sparks from the creative friction of diverse viewpoints. They seek team members who think differently, structure meetings to hear quiet voices, not just dominant ones. They welcome challenging questions. Importantly, their daily actions demonstrate that diversity accesses the full range of human creativity and wisdom needed to solve complex problems. In diverse environments, solutions emerge that no homogeneous team could discover.

Consider Madam C.J. Walker's success: She brought her diverse experience to solve a problem that leading businesses wouldn't and couldn't see. And she approached her ideal clientele where they were—in their homes. By stepping outside traditional models, she included those needing something different, presented uniquely. Traditional thinking would not have sufficed.

True leadership authenticity transcends superficial attributes, reaching deep within a leader's core where values, purpose, and action align. This alignment creates gravity that naturally draws others toward expressing their own truth. Teams solve problems more creatively because people feel safe offering unconventional ideas. Retention improves as employees experience work as an extension of their authentic selves rather than a mask they must wear. Innovation accelerates when diverse perspectives find welcome rather than resistance.

When centered in authenticity, leaders possess a strong foundation for decision-making, navigating challenges, and uplifting others. This represents a departure from scarcity mentalities, leading to growth within the leader, those who follow, and the entire organization.

Authenticity fosters trust, transparent communication, and inclusivity, creating an environment where success is shared and collective growth is celebrated. It is when leaders learn to embrace authenticity and embark on the transformative journey of self-discovery that they carve out a lasting impact.

REFLECTIONS

1. **Foundation Assessment:** Examine your leadership foundation. Where do you feel most solidly centered? Where do you sense instability? Consider how your authentic strengths might transform perceived weaknesses into unique advantages.

2. **Impact Evaluation:** Consider how your centered (or uncentered) state affects your organization. Where do you see your authentic leadership creating permission for others to step into their truth? Where might your guardedness be limiting team potential?

3. **Growth Edge Exploration:** Looking ahead, what aspect of Centered Leadership calls you to deeper development? Where do you need more guidance to fully embody Centered Leadership? What qualities would you seek in a coach or mentor who could help you recognize your blind spots and strengthen your authentic presence? Remember: Even the most Centered Leaders continue to seek guidance as their journey evolves.

CONCLUSION

CHOOSING CENTERED LEADERSHIP

In these brief chapters, we explored how traditional leadership models are giving way to more effective approaches—ones that embrace inclusivity, self-awareness, empathy, and adaptability. We've discovered that true leadership strength flows not from authority but from authenticity, not from control but from connection.

The most effective leaders operate from a stable center, where self-awareness meets purpose, where vulnerability creates strength, and where personal growth catalyzes organizational transformation. This centered approach prioritizes deep listening that transforms communication, emotional intelligence that builds trust, and inclusive practices that unlock innovation. These elements prove fundamental to long-term success, particularly in our rapidly evolving business landscape.

Embracing Centered Leadership requires a fundamental reimagining of how power flows through organizations.

Where traditional leadership created bottlenecks of authority, Centered Leadership releases energy throughout the system. This transformation begins in the leader's mindset, where scarcity thinking gives way to abundance, control yields to trust, and individual achievement expands into collective empowerment. While the old model often resulted in disengaged employees and limited growth potential, the centered approach recognizes the value of collaboration, open communication, and shared decision-making.

Centered Leadership creates environments where innovation naturally emerges because people feel safe to contribute their full potential. It builds cultures where diversity strengthens decision-making because different perspectives receive genuine consideration. Most importantly, it fosters workplaces where engagement soars because people bring their whole selves to their work.

Self-awareness forms the cornerstone of this fresh approach. Leaders who deeply understand their strengths, weaknesses, values, and biases navigate challenges with more clarity and intention. When leaders understand their triggers, they respond rather than react. When they acknowledge their biases, they make fairer decisions. When they know their strengths, they delegate more effectively. This self-knowledge creates the stability from which agile leadership naturally flows.

Equally crucial, empathy amplifies leadership impact by turning connection into competitive advantage. Centered Leaders read the emotional currents running through their organizations and channel this energy productively. They create psychological safety that encourages innovation. They build trust that speeds decision-making. They inspire their teams to go above and beyond. Leaders must be agile and willing to embrace change. They need to be open to new ideas, perspectives, and approaches.

Leadership development remains an ongoing quest. Madam C.J. Walker's rise from washerwoman to millionaire entrepreneur exemplifies how growth demands both perseverance and humility. Despite her unprecedented success, she continued seeking guidance from mentors and learning from her sales agents' experiences. "I got my start by giving myself a start," she famously said, but she never stopped growing, learning, or pushing beyond comfortable boundaries.

Today's Centered Leaders embrace this same commitment to continuous expansion and refinement. Maintaining a proper Center requires regular renewal through coaching, community support, and conscious practice. No leader, however accomplished, outgrows the need for feedback and fresh perspectives. The humility to remain coachable combined with the perseverance to keep evolving creates leadership that stands up and stands out.

There is no one-size-fits-all solution to fully embrace Centered Leadership. Each person's path looks different because each leader brings unique strengths, challenges, and aspirations to the journey. What unites Centered Leaders isn't their starting point but their commitment to continuous evolution. Creating a culture of acceptance and inclusion requires openness, introspection, and a great coach to meet the organization where it is, recognize its leaders' potential, and partner together toward a more equitable future.

These principles provide practical pathways to organizational transformation. In our personal and professional landscapes where change accelerates daily, and each week can be met with unforeseen and unprecedented conundrums, Centered Leadership provides both stability and adaptability. It creates deep roots that allow organizations to bend without breaking, innovate without losing their essence, and grow without sacrificing their values.

When leaders find their center, organizations discover their soul. Teams move from mere productivity to genuine creativity. Employees transform from merely checking off task boxes to purpose-driven contributors. The workplace shifts from a source of stress to a space of growth. These changes emerge through the natural influence of leaders who have done the inner work necessary to create outer change. In this way, Centered Leadership creates solutions for both the challenges of today's business environment and the deeper human longing for meaningful work.

Leadership transformation begins with a single step—the decision to lead from center rather than reactively, from authenticity rather than authority, from purpose rather than power. The She Center is your partner in this journey, offering community and coaching to turn leadership potential into impact. We provide the education we should have had from the start.

Consider these chapters not as closing pages but as an invitation to discover your unique leadership center, build organizations that thrive through authentic connection, and join a growing community of leaders transforming how power flows through the world. Your journey to becoming a Centered Leader begins now. The impact of your transformation awaits.

THE SHE CENTER

The She Center knows that a better world for women is a better world for everyone. We believe that the root of every problem we face, personally and globally, is the missing influence of women. Our mission is to restore women into leadership, decision-making, authenticity, personal peace, and power through the principles of Centering Self.

A transformative culture open to everyone, **The She Center** has empowered over 9,000 women since 2010 to break free from limitations, rewire old patterns, and design lives that feel as good as they look. Through neuroscience-backed coaching, aligned community, and proven principles, we support our community to accelerate their progress and take their healing journey from decades to days.

Our community celebrates profound outcomes including: financial abundance, unshakeable self-trust, emotional intelligence and mastery, expedited promotions, effective communication, freedom from disordered eating, rewritten generational patterns, healed relationships, and most importantly, an internal experience of

freedom, peace, and authenticity. **The She Center** is more than community, coaching, and personal growth; it is the reclamation of your influence, your innate freedom, and a purpose-driven future.

The She Center has earned recognition from major outlets like *The Wall Street Journal*, CBS, NBC, Fox News, Yahoo!, The Good Men Project, and beyond. We celebrate conducting leadership and communication trainings for the U.S. Army, Emmy award winners, those in Forbes' 50 Over 50, and for leaders at National Geographic, Disney, and Adobe, among others.

The She Center lives everywhere women are stepping into their power and gathers in online and in-person communities.

Find out more at theshecenter.org

GOOD MEDICINE PRESS

Where Stories are Sacred

Good Medicine Press publishes bold, soul-stirring works that challenge the status quo, honor ancestral knowledge, and open space for healing, truth, and transformation. We amplify underrepresented voices—particularly those of women, people of color, Indigenous storytellers, and historically marginalized communities—to uplift narratives that inspire a more just, connected, and equitable world.

We believe that reading words written in courage and authenticity is an act of liberation—one that helps deprogram internalized oppression and reclaim voice, power, and self. Every book we publish is an offering: a disruption of systems that harm and a celebration of resilience, community, healing, growth, and radical hope.

At **Good Medicine Press**, we publish books for a world where stories redefine what is possible, where diverse voices are centered, and where literature becomes a sacred force for restorative change.

Discover more at goodmedicinepress.com

GOOD
MEDICINE
PRESS